MARY

At My Side

Bob Guste

🏛
XXIII
TWENTY-THIRD PUBLICATIONS
Mystic, Connecticut

To
the other "Marys" in my life, beginning with my own mother,
who have reflected for me, each in her own way, the gen-
tle, strong, loving, and caring maiden of Nazareth, this little book is gratefully and lovingly dedicated.

Twenty-Third Publications
P.O. Box 180
Mystic, CT 06355
(203) 536-2611

Library of Congress Catalog Card Number 85-51277
ISBN 0-89622-247-0

Edited by Eleanor Buehrig
Designed by Andrea Star
Art by Gretchen Reid

Foreword

I for one am happy to welcome a new book about our Blessed Mother. I am especially happy because it is the result of Father Bob Guste's personal experience. Books which are the result of life experiences have a special value.

The campus on which I now teach is the same one I came to each day as a high school student. There is a statue of Mary on our campus. The inscription at its base reads "Behold your Mother." I feel a warm, nostalgic smile in my heart whenever I pass in front of the statue.

Through the years of my seminary training, Mary was never far away. She became my personal role-model of faithfulness. God had called her and she had said "yes." Whenever I see or think of the well known *Pietà* of Michelangelo, Mary holding her dead Son in her arms, I think of all the other "yeses" inside Mary's total surrender to God's will.

God had called me, too, and I had said my own "yes." There have been other "yeses" inside my own original commitment. I have been down in the valleys of my own weaknesses and failures. I have been high up on the mountains of transfiguration when I felt I could touch God's face. And with me always was the presence of Mary.

Somewhere in the transition of recent years, the Church seems to have lost some of its sense of Mary's presence. I suppose that in every move something is lost and has to be found again. In fact, some believe that we have to lose a thing of value and find it again to appreciate it fully.

I am grateful to Father Bob Guste for helping us to find again this most precious gift, the presence of Mary in our lives. She is indeed "our life, our sweetness, and our hope."

John Powell, S.J.
Loyola University of Chicago
May, Mary's Month, 1985

CONTENTS

And Mary pondered these things in her heart.

Luke 2:51

INTRODUCTION

Entering into a personal relationship with Jesus Christ was the single most important turning point in my spiritual journey. Countless persons have said and could say the same. Many have written about it beautifully, such as Fr. John Powell, S.J., in *He Touched Me* (Argus Communications, 1974). I've shared my story about finding Jesus in a new way while giving retreats, missions, and spiritual direction. One of these days I may write about it. But I want to share something different here: the story of discovering Mary, the mother of Jesus, and how she, in turn, helped me in my relationship with her Son.

Devotion to Our Blessed Lady is precious to most Catholics, to many other Christians, and even to some non-Christians. However, devotion to Mary is also a problem for many persons within or outside the Catholic Church who do not understand the reason for it and consider it an obstacle in their relationship with Our Lord Jesus Christ. This is especially true since the Second Vatican Council. Many misunderstood the message of the Council to be discouragement of devotion to Mary. Actually, the Council said nothing to that effect. On the contrary, the conclusion to its document on the Church devoted more space to Our Lady than any previous Council document in history. Vatican II did, however, strongly reaffirm the Church's understanding that Jesus Christ is central to all its devotional and missional life and that other devotions such as to Our Lady are meant ultimately to lead us to him, or more precisely, to the Father through him.

> There is but one Mediator as we know from the words of the apostle, "for there is one God and one mediator of God and man, the man Christ Jesus, who gave himself a redemption for all" (1 Tim. 2:5-6). The maternal duty of Mary towards men in no wise obscures or diminishes this unique mediation of Christ, but rather shows his power. For all the salvific influence of the Blessed Virgin on men originates, not from some inner necessity, but from the divine pleasure. It flows forth from the superabundance of the merits of Christ, rests on his mediation, depends entirely on it and draws all its power from it. In no way does it impede, but rather does it foster the immediate union of the faithful with Christ *(Constitution on the Church #60).*

There is one "mediator" between God and us — Christ Jesus — but, evidently, God uses many other "ambassadors for Christ" and he entrusts "the message of reconciliation to us" (2 Corinthians 5:19-20). He uses each of us to reach out to one another with love and prayer and the good news of Jesus. Powerfully, he used Peter and Paul and the other apostles; he used the prophets and saints from the beginning and down through the ages. Strikingly, in modern times, he continues to use Mary, his Mother and ours.

Because there were many years as a Catholic when I neither understood nor relished devotion to Our Lady, I can readily empathize with fellow Christians who have similar reactions. It is my desire to share with them the ways that God helped me in this regard.

Chapter I describes the first significant breakthroughs that occurred in my service as a major seminarian and newly ordained priest, which helped me understand the role of Our Lady. Chapter II relates the understanding that came to me years later about what Mary exemplified for me and for others who were called to respond to Jesus Christ. Chapter III develops ways that I was helped to accept the mystery of Mary as spiritual Mother. Chapter IV considers the personal impact of three of the renowned apparitions of Mary and their possible significance for us today. The final chapter briefly treats the rediscovery of the beauty and power of the rosary and other practices of devotion to Mary.

Many persons helped me with the text of this book — through information, constructive criticisms, and suggestions. Others gave time and care to typing and to correcting the manuscript, and there were those who offered encouragement and prayers for its completion and success. To all, I want to say from my heart — thank you.

Although this is not a book on theology, naturally some theology is involved in it. It is, nevertheless, the statement or testimony of one Catholic Christian about the role Our Lady played in his life. It is a love story that I tell; a song, a hymn of praise and joy I want — in my sometimes off-key voice — to sing of Mary. May it, with Mary's motherly intercession and inspiration, help many, especially you who are reading it right now as you continue your life's journey and mission.

CHAPTER I

A Prayer
in the Night

MY SONG, STORY, OR TESTIMONY of discovering Mary begins in my home city, New Orleans, when a serious accident endangered my oldest brother's life. My brother was snitching a chip of ice from the back of one of those old-time model A "ice trucks" that came through our neighborhood. It was something we kids would do. When the truck stopped and the "ice man" was toting the ice into a house, we would scramble upon the back of it to get ice chips for sucking. In summer it was always a big treat!

On this particular day, a car rounded the corner and struck my brother, Billy, tossing him in the air; and he landed on his head. In great concern and panic, the driver of the car picked him up and rushed him to a hospital. Hearing the noise of the small crowd outside, my mother, who was pregnant with me, came out of our house. She was told what had happened, but no one could tell her where Billy had been taken. After a number of frantic telephone calls, she located the hospital and rushed to it. Prepared for the worst, she entered the emergency room where he lay; and when she saw that he was alive, she knelt down in prayer. In her prayer, she promised Our Lady right then and there that she would say a rosary every day of her life in thanksgiving. Today, when my mother talks about the accident she still chokes up with deeply felt emotion. She's 89 years old now; and since her promise, she hasn't missed a day of praying the rosary.

Naturally, I grew up with exposure to the rosary and to devotion to Our Lady. In fact, the parish of my baptism and elementary schooling was Our Lady of Lourdes; and the Dominican nuns were my teachers. Despite this, personally, I had little or no devotion to Mary — not even during my years as a student for the priesthood, including years at the New Orleans major seminary, Notre Dame, which is named after Mary. The faculty of Marists was specially dedicated to her. In retrospect, I realize that one stumbling block in my devotional life was that my approach to God was cold, intellectual, and impersonal! Years later, when I was a young priest, an aged German nun hit the nail on the head. She told me: "The trouble with your sermons is that they're too cerebral. You've got to get more of your heart into them." (I didn't like it when you said it, but thanks, Sr. Theodosia!)

A statue of Our Lady stood at the foot of the large staircase that led to the second floor of the seminary. One custom of some students was to stop for a moment at the statue to say a little prayer to Mary before going up to their rooms after night prayers. One night about a year before ordination, I paused at the statue. What I said was something like this. "Look, Mary, I don't have any personal devotion to you. I don't see how you fit in with the whole deal — God's plan of salvation. It seems to me Jesus is enough. But I think I'm missing something and I'm asking you to pray for me to find it. Help me to understand."

Our Lady heard that prayer, and the answer came in God's own time. In fact, the answer keeps coming little by little as God unfolds to me the meaning of devotion to Mary.

The first breakthrough occurred one Sunday afternoon, some months after my prayer in the night, as we gathered around the old box-radio in a corner of the basement recreation room of the seminary. It came during the regular four o'clock Sunday afternoon broadcast of the brilliant Msgr. Fulton J. Sheen. In those days, his golden voice and moving messages captured the attention of millions of Americans of all faiths. On this particular Sunday his talk was on Our Lady. Of course, I don't remember the details nor even the main points. What I do remember is that he quoted a poem about Mary—a child's poem by Mary Dixon Thayer.

The poem bypassed my mind and went to my heart. Then it came back to my mind, and the meaning and significance of it clicked. In a flash I understood something of the role of Mary—that of leading us to Jesus. This poem might be "old hat" for many readers, but whether it is or not, I invite you to read it right now, slowly and meditatively, as if it were also your first time.

Lovely Lady dressed in blue
Teach me how to pray!
God was just your little boy,
Tell me what to say!

Did you lift him up, sometimes,
Gently, on your knee?
Did you sing to him the way
Mother does to me?

Did you hold his hand at night?
Did you ever try
Telling stories of the world?
O! And did he cry!

Do you really think he cares
If I tell him things—
Little things that happen? And
Do the Angels' wings

Make a noise? And can he hear
Me if I speak low?
Does he understand me now?
Tell me—for you know.

Lovely Lady dressed in blue,
Teach me how to pray!
God was just your little boy.
And you know the way.

The poem is not exactly a theological treatise! But it did speak to me and still does. It spoke so well that as a deacon in the seminary chapel, I used it in my first sermon for fellow students (and did I get razzed!).

The poem captures a deep truth in a child's language that the role of Our Lady is to lead us to her Son. The focus of the poem is not the Lovely Lady—but Jesus. It is a meditation on him as a child and on Mary's unique relationship with him, as his mother. It is a prayer addressed to her, who of all God's creatures was closest to Christ in body and spirit. It is a prayer asking by her example and intercession to help us to pray—to talk to Jesus simply and lovingly, with the heart of a child, and thereby share her intimate, personal relationship with him.

God used her as the instrument through which he came into the world, and through the ages he has used her to draw the world to himself. God could have done it another way, but he didn't; and it's important to understand his way.

This was strikingly brought home to me again about two years after ordination when my younger brother, a priest friend, his nephew and I all had the opportunity to go to Europe. In the midst of a whirlwind adventure, racing around in a little French Renault, seeing as much as we could in the short time at hand, we stopped at Lourdes in France. It proved to be one of the most memorable highlights of the trip. Typical of the kind of traveling we were doing, we arrived in the evening just in time to check into a little hotel, get something to eat, and rush over to the candelight procession which takes place at this hallowed shrine every night in season.

What I witnessed that evening was a dramatic, symbolic statement of the role of Our Lady in the life of God's people today. On that particular night I recall there was a large representation of servicemen from Great Britain in the procession, together with tens of thousands of people from all over France and other parts of the world. Slowly and with deep devotion, the crowds carrying candles marched their way around the grounds of the shrine singing, "Ave, Ave, Ave, Maria." The procession came to a halt in the square in front of the huge Lourdes basilica.

In one accord, the great crowd recited in Latin the Credo — the ancient creed that expresses the essentials of our faith in Jesus and in what he has revealed to us. Then, dramatically, the doors of the church were opened and God's people surged in to kneel in adoration before Our Lord in the Blessed Sacrament and receive his benediction. Mary was still gathering her children together from all corners of the earth to the feet of her Son.

Let it be done to me according to your will.

Luke 1:38

CHAPTER II

Type and Model
of the Church

PICK UP THE SCRIPTURES and read all the passages about Our Lady. As you meditate on them, you come to realize that in Mary you are contemplating a model or image of what you and I and the whole Church are called to be. This idea is central to Vatican Council II's statement on Mary and it is why it was included in its document on the Church. "... [Mary] is hailed as a pre-eminent and singular member of the Church, and as its type and exemplar in faith and charity" *(Constitution on the Church,* 54). However, a book by Hugo Rahner (brother of Karl), *Our Lady and the Church* (Pantheon Books, 1961) initially stimulated my thinking and praying along these lines. I began to see Mary in a new light — as the first Christian, the first to be touched by Jesus Christ in faith and in the flesh. If John can say in his prologue "any who did accept him he empowered to become children of God" (John 1:12), then Mary is the prototype of all who have accepted and will accept him till the end of time.

For example, the first passage of Luke's gospel gives the account of the Annunciation. "How can this be?" Mary asks, and the answer follows: "The Holy Spirit will come upon you and the power of the Most High will overshadow you." That passage is there not just to tell us something about Mary but to tell us something about ourselves. Any time God calls us to a task, to do anything in his name and we, like Mary, question how we can accomplish it, his answer is for us, as it was for her: "The power of the Most High will overshadow you. The Holy Spirit will come upon you ... for nothing is impossible with God" (Luke 1:35-37).

Mary's response is also for us. In my first parish assignment in downtown New Orleans, I was invited to Mrs. Eber's third grade classroom to witness a simple play the children had prepared. Since it was Christmastime, the play started with the Annunciation. A little boy was the angel and a little girl was Mary. The boy-angel came in all out of breath but still managed to blurt out: "Mary, God has chosen you to be his Mother." And the little girl answered: "OK!" As I've thought about her OK through the years and laughed about it, I realize more and more that that's all God is asking of every one of us: Just say "OK" every day to his will, embrace whatever he sends, put your heart into the call of duty and the demands and opportunities of each present moment.

The Visitation is another example (Luke 1:39-56). It's Mary reaching out to share the good news with another and taking care of the simple human needs of her pregnant cousin. It's Mary crying out a hymn of thanksgiving and praise. But it's there for us that we might do the same: Share Christ with one another and "help carry one another's burdens" and in that way "fulfill the law of Christ" (Galatians 6:2). Her song, too, is the song of the Church. The sacred writer is showing us Mary's heart and Mary's spirit and putting on our lips a hymn by which we can all praise the Lord until he comes again. Indeed it has become the great hymn of thanksgiving of the Church, sung every day and around the earth in vespers or evening prayer. Would that the spirit of that song stay in our hearts every hour and moment, as expressed in the chorus of the old hymn, "Blessed Assurance": "This is my story; this is my song: praising the Savior all the day long."

Mary, standing under the cross (John 19:25-27), is a sign of the disciple and symbol of the Church who takes seriously the injunction of the Master: take up your cross and follow me — faithful to the end. One of my first converts to the Catholic Church, with whom I've stayed in contact through the years, shared this with me. She said that even after being received into the Church, she still felt an inner barrier concerning devotion to Our Lady. Just about a year ago, however, her young son was in a serious accident. While in the hospital, waiting and watching at his bedside, she began to think about another mother, many centuries before, standing at the cross of her Son, and suddenly it happened: the wall came down and she felt at one with the Mother of Jesus and turned to her for understanding and strength.

Mary in the Cenacle (Acts 1:12-14), waiting in prayer with the apostles for the coming of the Spirit, is an image of her presence with the Church down through the ages, in good times and in bad, praying with us, strengthening us, urging us always to be open, renewed and empowered by his Spirit to go out and "renew the face of the earth."

The following are other passages about Our Lady which have deep meaning for us: giving birth to her child and welcoming the shepherds (Luke 2:1-18); remembering and reflecting "in her heart" (Luke 2:19, 51); offering him back to God in the temple and hearing the prophecy about her own part in his sacrifice (Luke 2:22-35); sharing in Egypt the plight of the refugees of the world (Matthew 2:13-18); observing the Jewish law and experiencing the pain of a missing child (Luke 2:41-50); rearing a Son in Nazareth who "was obedient" to her and her husband (Luke 2:39-40, 51-52); enjoying with him the fun of a wedding reception and interceding with him for the newly married couple (John 2:1-11). Again and again Mary is presented as an example to us, deeply involved in our human condition and in the divine plan of salvation through Jesus. With the "wise men" we, too, will find "the child with Mary his mother" (Matthew 2:11), and like Joseph we need "have no fear about taking Mary" with us on our life's journey (Matthew 2:11), to help us respond to and follow the Lord.

PRIVILEGES

All the privileges of Our Lady defined by the Church and flowing from the main privilege of being the Mother of God are gifts of the Lord, not just for Mary, but also for us. What was done for her, and in her, is a sign of what the Lord Jesus wants to do ultimately and eschatalogically for us all, his bride, his body the Church.

Carl Jung, the great psychiatrist who died in the 1960s, although not a Catholic, rejoiced exceedingly when he received the news about the Catholic Church's proclamation of the dogma of the Assumption of Our Lady into heaven. He was equally enthusiastic and supportive of the doctrine of the Immaculate Conception. To him these doctrines and the Church's proclamation of them were magnificent, bold affirmations of the goodness of human nature; of the power of good over evil; of the positive force of God at work in the world to overcome all that is negative; of the light that "shines on in darkness, a darkness that did not overcome it" (John 1:5).

For a long time the doctrine of the Immaculate Conception (and Mary's sinlessness) meant very little to me. In fact, it repelled me. [Strictly speaking the Immaculate Conception refers only to freedom from original sin, proclaiming that from the first instant of her own existence, Mary was especially graced by God. It is used here, however, in a broad sense to include her freedom from all sin throughout her life.] I would identify it with the white, marble, lifeless, and expressionless statues of Our Lady that I was familiar with. Someone who was immaculate and free of all sin seemed remote to me — (even though for many years I had trouble recognizing my own sinfulness — a problem common to our present age!) Such a person appeared inhuman, distant, unreal, cold, aloof. I could not identify with her. In time, I began to realize that it should be the other way around. What is it that separates us from one another, that dehumanizes us, that cuts us off from God and our brothers and sisters? It is sin. Sin dries up our hearts in selfishness, lust, and pride. Sin is negative. It is the absence of something meant to be there. That something is love. We are created for love: to love and to be loved. Sin is perversion — the twisting of our purpose, the frustration of our design, the squelching of our deepest yearnings.

Visualize someone *without* sin. That person would be warm, close to God and to all her brothers and sisters, alive, filled with love, approachable, nondefensive, open, unafraid, unselfish, and not self-seeking. What a truly beautiful human being she would be! That's what one poet called Our Blessed Lady: " . . . our tainted nature's solitary boast." And she, in turn, becomes our ally in the conquering of sin and in the healing of the effects of sin within us. The ancient prophecy of Genesis foreshadowed this role of Our Lady when the Lord said to the serpent, "I will put enmity between you and the woman, and between your offspring and hers; he will strike at your head, while you strike at his heel" (Genesis 3:15). The woman is involved in the battle with Satan, the battle in which her Son crushes his head.

Mary is involved first of all by her immaculate conception. It is the great sign of the total victory of Jesus Christ over sin — so total that sin never corrupted her for one instant, neither "original" nor personal sin. And the Church has always maintained that it was Christ's victory — the victory of his amazing grace. The work of a doctor is great when he heals an ailment; even greater when he prevents it. Mary needed a savior, needed Jesus, just as much as you and I do. In our case he saves us from the sin we contract and commit. In her case he saved her from contracting or committing it. Thus, she becomes the example for us of the power of God in Jesus Christ, to totally defeat the forces of darkness and evil. As someone has said, if you ever get discouraged in your struggle with sin or evil, just look at the Book of Revelation and see what the end of the story is: Jesus wins! In Mary's case, it's the beginning of the book! That's what the Immaculate Conception is all about. Jesus totally won in Mary. He conquered. He defeated the ancient enemy. He crushed his head. And the victory in Mary is not just for Mary but for us—the great sign of what he can do and wants to do in each of us who opens our life to him. His amazing grace that accomplished a perfect work in Mary with her cooperation is at work in each of us, transforming us by stages in the midst of our struggles as we continue to turn to him, rely upon him, and give ourselves to him. And he will confirm the victory for us in that eternal state of sinlessness, the bliss of endless life, the glorious sharing of his life "filled with enduring love" (John 1:14). How powerful is the invocation in time of temptation that Mary taught St. Catherine Labouré, "O Mary, conceived without sin, pray for us who have recourse to thee." As Karl Rahner puts it:

> From the very beginning the predestined integration of Mary's personal life with her office in redemptive history stepped forth from God into historicity: it is called the Immaculate Conception and as such is an object of our faith. That we ourselves are predestined to such an integration is not a matter of faith but of hope, not a fact established from the first but a goal of life, a possibility held out to us, a goal of our life that enters only by degrees into saving-history (*Servants of the Lord,* Herder and Herder, 1968, p. 106).

The Assumption is also for us. It is the Church's celebration of the mystery of resurrection, accomplished in Mary, by the power of the death and resurrection of the Lord—as a symbol of what we will share if we are faithful to Jesus. She has gone before us into glory, body and soul, to spur us on to victory, so that how she is and where she is, we may also be. In her, God's kingdom has come in fullness in this world and in the next.

> The dogma of the Assumption complements the dogma of the Immaculate Conception in the same way that the resurrection of Christ complements his crucifixion and life of sacrificial service to others.

Just as the Immaculate Conception was not merely a
personal privilege conferred upon Mary but a reality
bestowed in view of her role in the economy of salvation, so the Assumption is not merely a personal
privilege unrelated to the wider mission of her life.
Her union with God in Christ was unique from the
beginning. Her call to final union with God in
Christ, in the totality of her human existence (body
and soul), was also unique in the end. The dogma of
the Assumption asserts something about human existence in asserting something about Mary: that
human existence is bodily existence, and that we are
destined for glory not only in the realm of the
spiritual but in the realm of the material as well
(Richard McBrien, *Catholicism,* Winston Press, 1981
p.886).

Father, forgive them, for they know not what they do.

Luke 23:34

CHAPTER III

Bob, Here Is
Your Mother

ON A TRIP TO THE HOLY LAND in the summer of 1963, I visited the family of an Arab friend of mine, Abraham Rafidi, whom I had met at home in New Orleans. Abraham came into the sacristy one day after Mass when I was stationed in downtown New Orleans and asked to be received into the Catholic Church. As members of the Orthodox Church, his was the only Christian family in a totally Moslem village, about fifteen kilometers from Jerusalem. Before I left on my trip he had asked me to visit them and had written ahead to let them know I was coming.

From Jerusalem, I took one of those crowded, bouncing buses on a dusty road and got off at the town of Bireh in the district of Ramalla. Bireh is reputed to be the place where the pilgrims stopped to rest on their way from their annual Passover visit to the Holy City where Joseph and Mary discovered that Jesus was not with them. Asking directions from people in town, I found the Rafidi home.

I walked up the stairs to where his mother was seated on the front porch; she got up, threw her arms about me and said something in her own language. One of her sons who spoke English translated it for me: "When I see you, I see my son."

I've thought about those words many times. What they say to me is what I believe Our Lady says to each of us: "When I see you, I see my Son." She accepts and takes each of us to her heart with the love with which she accepted and took to her heart her only Son, Jesus. She sees and loves us in him and him in us.

An elderly nun told me this personal story. When she was a little girl, her mother died and her whole world collapsed. She felt that she would never be happy again. She was angry with God for taking her mother. One day she went to confession and told the priest how she felt. He told her to kneel at the Blessed Mother's altar and talk it over with Our Lady. As she knelt, she realized she still had a mother, and always would, one who loved her many times more than her earthly mother. The anger and sadness left her and the love of Mary, her mother, has stayed with her ever since.

When Our Lady of Guadalupe appeared to Juan Diego on Tepeyac hill in Mexico, some of the most beautiful words she spoke were, "Do not be troubled ... Do not fear ... Am I not ... your Mother?"

Many of us have heard the interpretation of the famous passage in St. John's Gospel when Jesus, dying on the cross, entrusts his mother into the care of the beloved disciple and then entrusts the disciple into the care of his mother. "In turn, he said to the disciple, 'There is your mother' " (John 19:27). For many ages, members of the Church have seen in this act of Jesus a symbolic meaning more significant than the immediate event. They have understood that Jesus is giving over his mother to his disciples, his Church, that she might spiritually care for them and take them into her heart and prayer. At the cross she becomes what the fathers of the Second Vatican Council acclaimed her, "Mother of the Church." Many of us have heard this over and over. The words are beautiful and meaningful, but they might leave us personally untouched and unmoved. To a great extent, that was the way it was with me. However, one day, not many years ago, I read those words again, and for the first time, I *heard* them. Silently, in the depth of my heart, I heard Our Lord saying: "Bob, here is *your* mother!" And from that day on I have accepted her in a new way into my life and hope to never let her go.

Some Scripture scholars, as Fr. George Montague, S.M., have studied the words of the gospel, "From that hour onward, the disciple took her into his care" (John 19:27). They maintain that "took her into his care" has a much deeper meaning than just providing a roof over her head or taking her into his home. The words mean: he took her for his own, took her into his life, made room for her in his heart. This is what you and I are invited to do. God does not force his gifts on anyone: his love, his grace, his eucharist, his mother. He offers them as gifts. It is up to us to receive or reject them. He offers us the gift of his mother. On the day that we actually take her into our home, our life, our heart, then she becomes *experientially* our mother.

Pope John Paul II, from the first time that he stood on the balcony of St. Peter's and addressed the crowds shortly after he was chosen, has called the world to give new attention to Our Lady. He spoke of her in that very brief and spontaneous address and soon the world came to know his unusual motto "Totus Tuus" — All yours, O Mary. This total consecration of ourselves to Our Lady is a secret of sanctity and power that our pope and many of the saints have discovered, and we are invited to share in it. In his first Holy Thursday letter addressed to bishops and priests around the world, John Paul II urged priests to place their priesthood in the hands and under the care of Our Blessed Lady, asking her to guard and keep us. Subsequently he called upon all God's people in every vocation and walk of life to do the same.

In 1982 Pope John Paul II traveled to Fatima and on May 13 consecrated the world and Russia (although without specific mention of the country) to the Immaculate Heart of Mary. This act, which came exactly a year after the attempt on his life, was seemingly in response to the request of Our Lady of Fatima—a request that several pontiffs before him had fulfilled. What was different about this, however, was that John Paul II did so in moral union with the bishops of the world. He had written to each of them prior to his journey to Fatima and asked them to join him in spirit in the consecration. For the feast of the Annunciation, March 25, 1984, he again communicated with fellow bishops requesting them to renew that consecration but this time publicly and in union with him. This collegial manner of consecration had been specified by Our Lady. Sr. Lucia of Fatima, who was one of the three children who witnessed the apparitions, is reported to have said about the pope's action: "It will have its effect, but it will depend on the greater or lesser fidelity of men to this consecration" (Exclusive Interview, *Soul Magazine,* July-August, 1982, p. 6). Our Chief Shepherd has led the way, but it is now up to us in our dioceses, institutions, religious houses, schools, parishes, homes, and individual lives to make the consecration and to live it.

There are many prayers and forms of consecration. It will be the responsibility of the individual or individuals involved to choose the one most personally appropriate. Basically, what we are doing in consecration is accepting the gift of Our Mother from the hands of Jesus Christ and placing ourselves under her maternal care that she might keep us close to her Son, conformed to his will and open, as she was, to his Spirit. We could intellectualize from here to doomsday about the value of this. Why consecrate ourselves to Our Lady? Why not just to the Lord? Ultimately it is to the Lord that we consecrate ourselves, but Our Lady helps us give it all to him, "to let go and let God," as she did. God gave her to us precisely to help us give ourselves back to him. Countless Christians before us, including saints, theologians, popes, and ordinary folks testify to the value and power of consecration to and through Mary.

In July 1982, the last month of my sabbatical, God touched my heart to make such a consecration. Years before, when I was a much younger priest, a crisis in my life prompted me to seriously think about leaving the priesthood and consider marriage. However, I rededicated myself and recommitted myself to the Lord and to the celibate life. For years I would consciously and regularly renew that commitment. In time I stopped doing that. Little by little, quietly and subtly, some vague nebulous kind of reservation crept into my heart and mind. I still wanted celibacy; I was still committed to living it, but in the back of my mind there was a little door opened or ajar. It was like saying, "Well, maybe one of these days, if the going gets too tough (or whatever), I might ask a dispensation from the vow." I hardly ever verbalized this and seldom even consciously thought it, but way back in my head I knew it was there. One of the last places I visited on sabbatical was the Bethany House of Prayer for priests north of New York City. There was strong, vibrant, and masculine devotion to Our Lady in that house. Consecration was promoted. I was only there a couple of days, but before I left I knelt in the presence of the small community of my brother priests and a bishop; and with them assisting me by their prayers, I placed myself and my priesthood in the care of Our Lady. This still did not close the door. I was not consciously deciding to close it but it was an important step. The next one took place about a week later as I was driving south through the hills of Virginia.

Should I make that recommitment of my whole self and renew that promise, come what may, to live the rest of my life as a celibate priest? Should I burn the bridges and just give it all? What a question to be asking at the age of fifty-five! Yet it was real for me. I struggled with this as I drove home; and as with Jacob and the angel, I felt the Lord struggling with me. One morning in prayer in a motel room along the way, I opened the Bible to a passage in the Old Testament that shook me. It said: "Even now do you not call *me*, 'My father, you who are the bridegroom of my youth'" (Jeremiah 3:4). It was that passage that made it click. God wanted me entirely for himself. He was calling me to surrender everything, close the door, let go, and let God. I decided to do it.

A little, white-framed, wooden church was in a neighboring town. I stopped by the rectory and asked the priest if I could go over to the church and offer Mass. He helped me get things ready. Alone, I offered the sacrifice and offered myself in it. After Mass, I knelt in front of the statue of Our Lady, asked the assistance of her prayers, and renewed the commitment I had made as a young subdeacon to live a celibate life for the rest of my days.

As I drove away through the hills, I felt as happy as a newlywed! I was singing and my heart was jumping for joy. I had taken the Lord again as my "portion and my cup" (Psalm 16:3) and the cup was overflowing.

For years I had not worn a medal, scapular, cross, or any religious symbol. I used to feel that I didn't need all that. "If you don't know I'm a Christian by the way I live," I thought, "then forget it." But after consecrating myself once again to Our Lady and putting my entire priesthood, ministry, and celibacy in her hands, God put it into my heart to take the scapular and put it back around my neck. When I wear it now I experience the power of it. It is but a symbol, but it is a powerful one. Every time I feel it, see it, kiss it, adjust it, it reminds me that I have a mother: that I'm a son of Mary, I'm in her care, I've consecrated myself to her and her Son and I'll never be alone.

Behold, there is your mother.

John 19:27

CHAPTER IV

The Signs
of the Times

IT IS CHARACTERISTIC of many modern Catholics to ig-
nore or make little of apparitions of Our Lady, even those that
have been examined thoroughly by the Church and been found
worthy of credence. Yet, this is so in an age when all around
us there is a preoccupation with the bizarre, ESP, Eastern
mysticism, the diabolic, outer-space, and so on.

   Having emerged from a training that concentrated
heavily on the powers of human reasoning, I remember as a
young priest "scratching off" or readily discounting stories that
individuals would tell me about extraordinary and miraculous

happenings in their lives—especially when visions or voices were seen or heard. There is, of course, a schizophrenic phenomenon of hearing voices or alcoholic and other drug reactions that include hallucinations. And there are those who, to say the least, have "a too lively imagination."

Excepting these cases, there are enough persons who are normal and sane who will recount maybe but one extraordinary experience of God in their lifetime. Now, when I hear such a story at least I listen, admitting to the possibility of genuineness. I think that the writings of Morton Kelsey, especially his book *Encounter with God* (Bethany House, 1972), helped me with this. Kelsey writes that if we went through the New Testament and gutted all references to extraordinary experiences of God (including miracles, visions, dreams, etc.) we would find but half of it left! It is our super-intellectual and materialistic mind-set which conditions us to expect God to communicate himself to us only through intellectual reasoning; God's communications are often through experiences of himself.

Long ago, God's prophet Joel foretold that in the days of the Messiah, "I will pour out my spirit upon all mankind. Your sons and daughters shall prophesy, your old men shall dream dreams, your young men shall see visions; even upon the servants and the handmaids, in those days, I will pour out my spirit" (Joel 3:1). Jesus himself promised that "Signs like these will accompany those who have professed their faith . . ." (Mark 16:17), and he pointed to the signs that accompanied his own mission to verify that he was the one who was expected: "Go back and report to John what you hear and see: the blind recover their sight, cripples walk, lepers are cured . . . and the poor have the good news preached to them" (Matthew 11:4-5).

If miraculous signs are meant to confirm the preaching of the gospel, then why should we not accept those special apparitions that have been attested to by a thorough examination of ecclesiastical authority, by an extraordinary holiness of life on the part of the visionaries, by their consistency of narration even in the face of threats, and until the time of death and by a continuance of miracles over the years down to our own day?

For some time in my own life, especially during the later sixties and the seventies, I generally shied away from mentioning apparitions in my homilies and instructions. I find myself now, however, referring to them more often. I think they have a special relevance for our day. First of all, they call us back to many simple practices and truths of faith often neglected or ignored. Secondly, the apparitions hold up before us that essential disposition for receiving God's word and entering his kingdom: humility of heart or childlikeness. "What you have hidden from the learned and the clever, you have revealed to the merest children" (Luke 10:21). Most of the apparitions, especially the most famous of them, were to the poor, the humble, and children, the "little people" of the earth. Thirdly, the three most famous of the approved apparitions of Our Lady have a very timely relationship with the present day yearnings for spiritual renewal, healing of mind and heart and spirit, human dignity, justice, and world peace. Finally, the apparitions strikingly demonstrate that it is the plan of God to intimately involve his Mother in the salvation and welfare of the entire human family.

LOURDES

In the summer of 1982, I visited the shrine of Our Lady of Lourdes in France. It was part of a six-month sabbatical that had been granted to me after 32 years of parish ministry in preparation for a new work of spiritual renewal involving parish missions, retreats, days of recollection, etc. I had been to Lourdes 30 years earlier. This time I went with the black gospel choir from my last pastorate at St. Francis de Sales Church in New Orleans. I wanted to put my new ministry under the care of our Blessed Lady.

What I witnessed was the continual "miracle of Lourdes," which goes on year after year. To this little town from all over the world millions of people come every year as pilgrims, possibly more than to any other spot on the earth, including Jerusalem, Mecca, and Rome. They come because of Our Lady and her appearances to a simple peasant girl, Bernadette. They come, drawn by Mary, but drawn to her Son.

We were at Lourdes only one evening. We arrived just in time for the afternoon procession of the Blessed Sacrament for the sick. The sacrament of the Body of Christ is the center of this procession. Most of the physical healings that are documented and substantiated at Lourdes happen during Our Lord's blessing of his people in and with this sacrament.

A number of us took part that evening in the candlelight procession. At the evening procession, it is announced over the loudspeakers that the candles are symbols of Jesus, the Light of the World. As the procession wends its way around the grounds, the participants sing hymns and recite the rosary, both interspersed with meditations on the life of Our Lord. Then it stops in front of the basilica, and the entire assembly recites together the Creed, the expression of our Christian/Catholic faith.

Frequently during the day, Mass is offered and throngs of people attend and receive Holy Communion. Throughout the day the special "reconciliation chapel" is open; it is continually occupied and confessions are heard in many different languages. The miracle of reconciliation with the Lord and his Church is being renewed over and over. In all these ways, Mary is gathering her children together from all corners of the world and bringing them to her Son through the Church.

As I left that shrine early the next morning on a crowded bus for the return trip to Paris, there was a message from the Lord that was ringing in my heart. He was saying, "Look, if you're interested in spiritual renewal, *don't neglect my mother.* I'm using her to bring my people back to me and to deepen their lives in me." That message is one of the main reasons for this booklet.

After that visit to Lourdes I re-read the life of Bernadette. This time the biography was written by René Laurentin. The preface of the French edition says this about the author: "After twenty years of study and twenty-five volumes of scientific publications as his authority, Abbé René Laurentin, professor at Catholic University, Doctor of Letters, but also journalist, has written a life as transparent and simple as Bernadette according to the instruction which she gave historians on her deathbed. 'The simpler one writes, the better. In an effort to embellish, one distorts'." I loved Laurentin's book, and recommend it to everyone. Above all, I loved it because it is evident that there is no exaggeration in it or effort to impress. He writes with the accuracy and honesty of a newspaper reporter and historian who is hunting for "just the facts." Through its pages, Bernadette comes across as completely disarming the priests and government interrogators by her utter simplicity, lack of sophistication and guile. She was beautifully and painfully honest and consistent about her story until the end of her life.

One of the great revelations to Bernadette by Our Lady was her name (reminiscent of God revealing his name to Moses). Our Lady said, "I am the Immaculate Conception." Bernadette did not understand what she was saying, but she reported it just as she had heard it. Those to whom she told it, "the learned and the clever," said that the Lady could not have said that because it did not make sense. Bernadette held to her story and the words remain. What is the importance of that title and its meaning for us today? I have already written something about this in Chapter II but a few more comments might be added here.

The Immaculate Conception is about sin — complete freedom from sin through the power of God — whereas the world we live in is characterized by the loss of the sense of sin and an attitude of helplessness in the face of much that used to be called sin.

Psychologists have learned that there are unconscious forces at work in all of us that influence our actions and conscious pressures in society that do the same. However, unless we are completely deranged, we remain basically free. Most say "yes" or "no" to temptation; most know right from wrong. We are responsible for our actions.

One of Europe's eminent psychiatrists, Viktor Frankl, in his book, *Man's Search for Meaning* (Beacon Press, 1959), upholds this truth about out basic freedom. His experience in a Nazi concentration camp showed him that men and women are able to act out of their own inner freedom no matter what pressures come to them from without and from within. The Immaculate Conception reminds us that the power of sin and evil is real but the power of good and the power of God are more real. "Where sin abounded, grace did more abound" (Romans 5:20, Douay Version).

Throughout the Christian world today, there is renewed interest in healing and restoration through prayer — physical, spiritual, and psychological. In these areas, Mary has played and continues to play a powerful role. For ages Lourdes has been known as a center for healing, because of the remarkable, miraculous physical cures. These have been examined and attested by a famed medical bureau of doctors not only of all faiths but sometimes those of no faith. Yet the spiritual and psychological cures at Lourdes are the ones that appear to be unheralded and unnoticed. It is said that seldom does anyone go away from the shrine untouched in some way by the Lord — wanting to live a better life, experiencing the strength to do so, or just feeling their spirit uplifted through the intercession of a loving Mother. But however desirable and admirable it is to visit shrines like Lourdes, increasingly persons are coming to realize that the power of Mary's intercession is with us anywhere and always. I believe the Immaculate Conception is uniquely connected with the ministry of inner healing, especially that known as "the healing of memories." Countless persons suffer from memories, whether conscious or subconscious, adverse and unloving things that happened in their past, as far back as childhood or even at the beginning of life in the womb. Psychiatrists and psychologists tell us that *in utero* the child begins to pick up vibrations from the mother and her surrounding environment of love or lack of love, care or disinterest, acceptance or rejection, security or fear, joy or sadness, peace or anxiety. Mary, in her Immaculate Conception, is given to us as one who is completely healed — one penetrated to the core by God's love even from her mother's womb so that she, in turn, might become an inspired emissary for deep healing of us all. In her book *The Gift of Inner Healing* (Word Books, 1976, Ch. 4), Ruth Carter Stapleton, who was not a Catholic, demonstrates one or two striking examples of how Our Lady entered the imaginative memories of people for whom she prayed, persons who needed a mother's love at critical points or for periods of time in their lives. Mary is our mother and is thus a sign or "sacrament" of God's motherly care for us. She has been our mother all of our life, but when we were infants, and at many other periods of our lives, we may not have realized this truth. To consciously invite her into our memories when we need a mother's or a sister's love can be a great means of healing and restoration.

GUADALUPE

For many in the United States the story of Our Lady of Guadalupe is little known. I consider it, however, the most outstanding and striking of all the apparitions of Our Lady. The origin of this devotion is that Our Lady appeared December 9, 1531, which in those days was the time of the Feast of the Immaculate Conception, on a barren hilltop five miles north of Mexico City to an Aztec Indian convert, Juan Diego, who was on his way to an early morning Mass in her honor. The beautiful maiden told him that she was "the ever-holy virgin Mary, mother of the true God" and asked that he go to the bishop and request that a chapel be built on the spot as a place where she could manifest her maternal love for all her people.

The bishop, of course, was not ready to accept the story without some proof or sign which he told Juan to ask of the Lady if she returned. When he made the request, she instructed him to pick flowers from the top of the hill. It was winter, and flowers would ordinarily not be in bloom. To his amazement, Juan found a beautiful profusion of flowers, including Castilian roses. He carefully gathered them into his *tilma,* a type of rough mantle worn by many Indian men. He brought them to the bishop, and dropped them at his feet. The bishop and those in his company fell to their knees. For there, on the *tilma,* was a magnificent image of the Lady in beautiful striking colors!

The image, which still hangs over the main altar of the always crowded Basilica of Guadalupe in Mexico (which I visited years ago) has been examined by numerous artists and scientists.

Their conclusion is that the image surpasses the capabilities of execution by any human hand. Careful scientific study of the mantle reveals that because it was woven from the fibers of a maguey cactus plant, the mantle should have disintegrated within twenty to thirty years. Yet it has remained intact and strikingly beautiful for four and a half centuries! "And this despite the fact that for over a century the sacred image hung unprotected, even by glass, in a damp open-windowed chapel the size of an average living room where it was directly exposed to ceaseless smoke and incense, burnt perfumes, and the myriads of votive candles flickering beneath it." (Francis Johnson, *The Wonder of Guadalupe,* Tan Books and Publishers, Inc., 1981, Chapter VII "The Verdict of Science," Page 117).

These apparitions took place in the early stages of missionaries' efforts to bring the gospel to the people of the new world. Their efforts had borne little fruit up to the time the apparitions occurred, but then, with the simple telling of the story by Juan Diego and others, and with the miraculous healings that confirmed the account, countless streams of pilgrims began to come to the shrine. Eight million converts were made by 1538. It is estimated that the *number* would be about *3000* converts a day. Since the Scriptures say of the first Pentecost that "some three thousand were added that day" (Acts 2:41) — it was like a new Pentecost every day for seven years! (cf. Farrell and Kosicki, *Mary's Role in the New Pentecost,* AMI Press, 1981, Page 58). Our Lady once again was bringing her children to her Son through and in his Church.

The great missionary impact of these apparitions is meaningful for our times when there has been a lessening in missionary zeal. In an ecumenical age and an age that has a new awareness of the social implications of the gospel, it is important to be reminded that the greatest treasure God is calling us to share with the world is still "the unfathomable riches of Christ," the power of his Spirit, and the fullness of truth and life offered us "through the church" (Ephesians 3:8 and 12).

When Our Lady appeared to Juan Diego, she came as an Indian maiden, thus giving the people of the land an image they could identify with. Our Lady of Guadalupe subsequently was accepted as patroness of Mexico City, then of all Latin America, and finally Pope Pius XII in 1945 designated her as "Empress of the Americas." This title recognizes that at the time of the apparitions there were no divisions among North, South, and Central America; it was one land. Today when much of Latin America is in such agony and ferment, we can join our brothers and sisters below the border in invoking Our Lady of Guadalupe for the continued promotion of the gospel of Jesus and its infleshment in terms of human dignity, justice, and peace.

FÁTIMA

Finally, I want to say something about Our Lady of Fátima. I remember vividly the visit I made in 1952 to the shrine of Fátima in Central Portugal and to the home of the parents of Jacinta and Francisco Marto, who, with their cousin Lucia, were the children who saw Our Lady in the apparitions of 1917. The utter simplicity and poverty of the parents and their home, a small thatched-roof house with a dirt floor, remain with me to this day. We arrived when they were seated around the fireplace having their evening meal of a bowl of porridge. We talked and laughed with them through a Portugese interpreter and experienced their warmth and hospitality. As we left, I took a picture of the old man who came out to the road with us to bid us farewell, still holding his bowl in his hand. It was evident that they had derived no material profit from the fame of their children.

The apparitions at Fátima were attested by the outstanding miracle of the sun witnessed by over seventy thousand people, but there had been other signs before that. The miraculous courage of the three children who had been imprisoned and threatened with slow death by burning to induce them to change their story was also a sign of their veracity.

Fátima is significant because it relates to the peace efforts of our day. Our Lady gave us in 1917 (and in subsequent apparitions to Lucia) her "peace plan" from heaven. That plan includes prayer, sacrifice, conversion of life, consecration to her, and the first Saturday observance in reparation to her Immaculate Heart. She promised that if her requests were heeded, a time of peace would come upon the world. If not, Russia would spread its errors far and wide, another worse war would ensue, countries would be annihilated, and the pope would suffer greatly.

Fátima is significant also because it contains a confirmation and affirmation of some important truths of our faith that are frequently downplayed in the Church today. One of the most impressive apparitions at Fátima was the vision of hell which depicted the torments of the damned. Our Lady asked for prayer and sacrifice that souls would be saved from damnation, and she gave the children a prayer to say after each decade of the rosary: "O My Jesus, forgive us our sins; save us from the fires of hell; lead all souls to heaven especially those most in need." I don't like to think about hell any more than anyone else. I'm not a hell-fire damnation preacher. But the words of Our Lord, according to the Scriptures, speak of hell about 15 times and Our Lady reminds us about what our faith proclaims. God offers his grace even to the last breath of life, but it is possible in human freedom to reject his gift and be separated from him forever. Many seem to be on that road: "The gate that leads to damnation is wide, the road is clear, and many choose to travel it. But how narrow is the gate that leads to life, how rough the road, and how few there are who find it!" (Matthew 7:14).

Our Lady also said something to the children concerning purgatory. When they inquired about two persons who had died and whether or not they were in heaven, Mary answered, "One was, but the other was in purgatory."

Fátima likewise calls to our attention the spirit world of angels and devils; the latter were included in the vision of hell and the "angel of peace" appeared several times to the children at Fátima in preparation for the apparitions of Our Lady.

It is at Fátima that Mary called herself the Lady of the Rosary — confirming this long-standing Catholic devotion. Our Lady also appeared holding what Lucia understood to be a scapular, re-emphasizing a sacramental that many (including myself until recently) think outmoded.

Of special interest and importance is the request of Our Lady for the establishment of devotion to her Immaculate Heart and the observance of the five first Saturdays, which specifically includes the confession of our sins to a priest. Monthly confession was a regular ritual for many Catholics years ago, but there has been a drastic decline in this practice. It appears logical that Our Lady hopes that once we keep the five first Saturdays, a good habit might be started that will continue throughout our lives.

The overriding message of Fátima was a call for penance and sacrifice offered for the salvation of the world. The penance or repentance asked for is mainly that we turn away from sin. The sacrifice is primarily to perform our daily duties, faithfully. Put simply, Our Lady seemed to endorse praying and living the "morning offering," promoted so widely through the Apostleship of Prayer — the daily offering of our lives and everything in them: our joys, works, sufferings, and responsibilities.

One of the last things that I did when on sabbatical a couple of summers ago was to make an unplanned visit to Washington, N.J., to talk with John Haffert who has devoted forty-six years of his adult life to the study of the Fátima apparitions and to the propagation of its message. Most important he shared with me an interview he had had with Sr. Lucia when he asked her what she considered the significant part of the Fátima message. This interview as described in his recent book *Dear Bishop* follows:

> She (Sr. Lucia) went on to explain that the essential request of Our Lady of Fátima was conveyed to the three children in the very first question Our Lady put to them when she said, "Will you be willing to accept whatever God will send you and to offer it up for the conversion of sinners and in reparation for the offenses committed against the Immaculate Heart of Mary?" Over and over again during those precious hours I was in her company, she emphasized that it is the fulfillment of one's daily duty, according to one's state in life (and the sanctification of this effort in reparation for our sins and for the conversion of

sinners) which is the primary condition for the turning back of the tide of evil which threatens today's
world and which will also bring us the great favor of
the conversion of Russia and an era of peace for
mankind."
(AMI International Press, Washington, N.J. p.6)

Just do each day, each hour, each moment what you
are called to do. What a simple, yet profound; easy, yet dif-
ficult, message! Our Lady is asking a conversion of life and
a change of heart. She is asking that each of us, in whatever
walk of life we find ourselves, examine our station, vocation,
occupation, ask ourselves how Our Lord would have us live;
and then with all our heart, soul, and strength live fully,
wholeheartedly, and lovingly for God and our neighbor. We
are called to offer our lives in union with the offering of Jesus
to the Father for the salvation of the world. This offering is
renewed sacramentally every day, every hour, every moment
in some part of the world in the sacrifice of the Mass.

. . . and Mary herself shall be pierced with a sword.

Luke 2:25

CHAPTER V

You and Our Lady

I HAVE NEVER BEEN MORE CONVINCED that central to Christian life is the proclamation of the Lordship of Jesus Christ and the daily dying to self so that he may become more and more the Lord of our lives. I am also more convinced than ever that Our Blessed Lady has a God-planned place in the work of "restoring all things in Christ" and proclaiming him as Lord of all the earth, of every institution and aspect of our lives.

There are three chief practices that are traditionally associated with devotion to Our Lady: the rosary, the scapular, and consecration. I have held onto the rosary even during those many years when the devotion meant little to me. The

Dominican Sisters taught us that it was a good practice to carry the rosary in pocket or purse. Even if you are not saying it, it is a reminder of the Lord and Our Lady. At one of the parish missions I preached in Mississippi, a man gave this testimony: "For ten years I left the Catholic Church. In those years I tried to hate my Church. I went to many other churches. Eventually I returned for two reasons. The first was that in none of the other churches did I find the same kind of respect, reverence, and belief in the Holy Eucharist that I found in the Catholic Church. The second reason was because in all those years, I kept a rosary in my pocket. I don't know why I did it. I just couldn't get rid of it. And I believe it was my Mother who brought me home."

Personally, I feel that I am just learning how to say the rosary. The secret is: Slow down! So many of us race through the prayers of the rosary in private and communal recitation and thereby miss much of its beauty and power. It is interesting that one of the first things that Our Lady's visit at Fátima instilled in the children was how to pray it properly. It is especially in the rosary that the power of the names and images of Jesus and Mary can touch and take root in our souls. These are the principal words in the Hail Mary. The meditation on the mysteries also fills our minds and souls with Christ in most of the significant aspects of his life and mission. "Let this mind be in you which was in Christ Jesus," or as the New American translation puts it, "Your attitude must be that of Christ" (Philippians 2:5).

Psychiatrist Carl Jung says that the mental images of Jesus and Mary have unique power for influencing us toward good and overcoming the negativity with which we are all bombarded. At one parish mission an elderly gentleman, who is a leader in his community, shared the following experience.

> One night you asked us to open our hearts to Jesus and express to him the deepest desire of our hearts. Usually when I pray I pray for other people. That night I did something different. For many years my wife and daughter and I have been praying the family rosary. After the mission that evening, when we were praying the rosary something happened.

Somewhere during the rosary while I was saying the words "blessed is the fruit of thy womb, Jesus" that name began to come alive for me and I experienced Jesus' presence in a way I had not experienced him for years. You know I constantly struggle with a lot of things on my mind that trouble me and rob me of peace. Somehow as I repeated the name of Jesus with each Hail Mary all these things faded away and his peace came to me.

I have already said something about the scapular from a personal standpoint. The Church has approved the wearing of the medal in place of the cloth scapular but the former is still preferred. For many years as a pastor I had abandoned the practice that was prevalant in the days when I was young of giving the scapular around the time of first Holy Communion. Now I not only see the value of that (either then or somewhat later) but feel that the occasions of parish missions or retreats are opportune times to offer the scapular and/or miraculous medal again for those who have forgotten about them. The design for the miraculous medal was given by Our Lady to St. Catherine Labouré. The medal is inscribed with the powerful prayer: "O Mary, conceived without sin, pray for us who have recourse to thee." Both the scapular and the miraculous medal are signs and reminders of consecration to Our Lady. It is that consecration and the daily living of it that is especially desired by her for the transformation of souls and the conversion of the whole world.

Our devotion to Mary should never lack spontaneity and creativity. For example, occasionally I have imagined dropping in on Our Lady, sitting down at a table and having a cup of tea with her. These encounters and conversations have been rich experiences for me and have left lasting impressions. I remember one in which I imagined myself in the house at Nazareth. Jesus wasn't home at the time, but Mary and I had a talk. She told me, "My Son has often spoken to me about you." It was a touching experience of Jesus' and Mary's personal knowledge of and love for me.

My being proclaims the greatness of the Lord.

Luke 1:46

In the beautiful little book *Tales of a Magic Monastery* by Theophane the Monk there is this fanciful story:

> When the guestmaster asked me what my spiritual practice was, I told him, "The Rosary. I've been saying that every day for years. I have a great devotion to our Lady."
> "Would you like to meet her?" he asked.
> "What do you mean?"
> "Well, she's right over there, the door at the end of the cloister."
> "You mean I could have an appointment?"
> "No appointment, just go in." I did.
>
>   There she was, no mistaking it. She remained in her chair, but her eyes and face embraced me as if I were her infant. Then she spoke my name. That surprised me. Why did that surprise me, when I had been praying to her for so many years? I was speechless. She took my head to her heart.
>
>   Then after a bit she began to speak. It was reminiscing. She went back to my infancy, told me about my parents, my childhood, adolescence, then went right up to the present. But she saw it all so differently. It was a total reinterpretation of my life. Finally, she said, "Before you go, I want to give you something. It's my Amen. You'll find it very handy. You can use it in all sorts of situations. You can apply it to persons and memories. It will grow with use, and hopefully someday you will say the Great Amen."
>
>   I live now in the embrace of those eyes. Daily I use her Amen. Please pray for me that some day I may dare to say the Great Amen (Crossroad Publishing Co., New York, N.Y. p. 71).

I recently underwent major surgery in a local hospital. It wasn't very serious, but when you are operated on and anesthetized, you do think about the possibility of death. I said I wasn't afraid but I didn't sleep the night before! During that night while praying I turned my chair in the direction facing where I thought the parish church might be and ended my prayer with attention and reverence to Our Lord who is present in the tabernacle of that church. As the sun came up I was touched deeply when I noticed that right in view outside of my window in the direction I had faced the night before was the red-tile roof of Our Lady of Lourdes Church. It was there that I had been baptized as an infant, received my first Holy Communion, was confirmed, and offered my first Mass as a priest. It was to that church that my mother, who was pregnant with me, had gone to give thanks for sparing my brother's life those many years ago. It filled me with a great sense, not only of God's presence and care, but also of the presence at that moment of Our Lady who had accompanied me all my life's journey.

As the jolly green giants came in to roll me away to the operating room, I thought of that last journey which ultimately we all make alone, in which there will be no one else except Our Lord — and Mary and the saints — to assist us in the final surrender to the Father — the Great Amen. Amen means, yes, Lord, OK, what you will, what you want, what you are calling me to do: Amen. Every day and every moment you and I are called to say it. But it's all preparing us for the final Amen, the total surrender when we bow our heads, give it all, and say with Jesus, "Now, it is finished" (John 19:30), "Father, into your hands I commend my spirit" (Luke 23:46).

Holy Mary, Mother of God, pray for us sinners now and at the hour of our death. Amen!